One Child, One Planet

Inspiration for the Young Conservationist

by BRIDGET McGOVERN LLEWELLYN

photographs by CARL R. SAMS II & JEAN STOICK

Author's Acknowledgments

Special thank you to Carl R. Sams II and Jean Stoick, for believing in this project
and lending their inspirational photography to bring the words to life;
and for their guidance throughout the creation of this book;
Karen McDiarmid, for her enthusiasm and creative insight;
Bruce Montagne, Hugh McDiarmid, Kirt Manecke, Herb McHarg, Greg Dunn & Henry Pollack,
for sharing their expertise.

Thank you for your support: Linda Guldi, Ruthann McMath, Kathy Finneran, Anne Galovich,
Melanie Koehn, Coco Hildebrand, Kelly Smith Cotter, Carrie Parker, Mike & Connie Thompson,
Becky Ferguson, Mark & Beth Meacham, Jo Tarling,
Pat, Bridget, Mary Ellen, Patrick & Maureen McGovern

And last, but never least, Pat Llewellyn for your constant love and support,
and for playing outside with our young conservationists – Katelyn, Meghan, Claire & Audrey.

Emerald Shamrock Press LLC
P.O. Box 210704, Auburn Hills, Michigan 48321   (248) 860-9221
www.onechildoneplanet.com

Book design by Karen McDiarmid.
Color expertise by Greg Dunn of Digital Imagery.

Printed and bound October 2009, #46346,
Friesens of Altona, Manitoba, Canada.

Llewellyn, Bridget McGovern
One Child, One Planet: Inspiration for the Young Conservationist
by Bridget McGovern Llewellyn
Illustrated by Carl R. Sams II & Jean Stoick

Summary: One child learns about greenhouse gases, climate change,
going green and how conservation can protect Earth's environment.

ISBN 978-0-984-1880-0-0

1. Climatic changes – Juvenile Literature
2. Environmental protection – Citizen participation –
   Juvenile Literature
3. Global warming – Juvenile Literature
4. Greenhouse effect, atmospheric – Juvenile Literature
5. Ecology – Juvenile Literature

Library of Congress Control Number: 2009934949

10 9 8 7 6 5 4 3 2 1

For Katelyn, Meghan,
Claire & Audrey.
— B.M.L.

For those who shall inherit the Earth.
— C.S. & J.S.

As sure as the sun will shine,
as sure as the moon will glow,

we need Earth,
and Earth needs us,
more than we'll ever know.

"What is Earth?" you kindly ask.
"Why is it something I need?"

The answer is simple, my child.
Earth is home to the
air we breathe.

Earth is an ideal environment
for people, animals and plants

to live together, side by side,
in peace and perfect balance.

So far as scientists know,
Earth is a special place.

As mankind's favorite planet,
we should treat her with
kindness and grace.

Greenhouse gases protect our Earth
like a blanket in the sky.
This keeps our planet's climate right,
with temperatures not too high.

Though we need some greenhouse gases,
we don't want levels to grow.
Earth's climate can change and get warmer
in places that need lots of snow.

A bit of trouble
lies ahead:
climate change needs
our consideration.
We tend to waste
power and resources.

It is time for CONSERVATION!

"Earth, so big, and me, so small —
Oh, what good can I do?"

Funny you should ask, my child.
The world's been waiting for you!

There's been talk about "going green"
    (the most beautiful color we know).

  If we don't "go green,"
in all we do,
    we may see less
        ice and snow.

Think we wouldn't miss the snow?
The Arctic climates too cold?
We need some freeze to tame the high seas
and protect our glorious world.

Without icebergs and Arctic air,
    ocean levels and temperatures climb.

Penguins and polar bears
    lose their homes.
Coastal beaches recede
    over time.

We say, "Go Green!"
yet mean, "Go White!"

Save the ice caps.
Prevent
global warming.

Go green!
Go white!

Go **RAINBOW** of **COLORS**!

The movement is soon
to be swarming!

Three big favors Mother Earth asks:

Reduce,
Reuse,
Recycle.

*"How can I make
a difference?"*
you ask.

Explore ways
to change
your
lifestyle…

Water, a most precious resource,
vital to all living things,
is something that shouldn't be wasted.
Don't let it run down the drain!

Whether bathing,
brushing your teeth,
or washing
your hands
or dishes,
try doing so
with less
water.

*"I'll save it
for the fishes!"*

Trees promote
healthy living
by cleansing the air
we breathe.

They take out
carbon dioxide and
provide oxygen,
so clean.

Earth's tall trees bear many gifts —
   cool places with breathtaking views.
To properly care for healthy air,
   we replenish by planting anew.

Paper can be recycled.
We can use both front and back.
Send e-mail greetings instead of cards.
When shopping, bring reusable bags.

We can each save electricity
by turning off lights in the house.
Limit time on electronics.
Play outside. Get off the couch!

Help your family recycle
things like paper, plastic and glass,

bottles, cans
and outgrown clothes,
fallen leaves
and clippings
of grass.

You may have items here and there,
no longer of use to you.
Someone else might find them nifty.
Usefulness can be renewed!

Simplify. Buy less "stuff"
while shopping at the store.
Buy just what you need. Squash any greed.
Do you really *need* any more?

Most importantly, young and old —
we must be keenly aware
of the awesome-ness
that surrounds us,
and treat it
all with care.

For if we all work together
and each of us does our share,
we can make our space a happy place
by keeping clean our air.

Just like Mom likes a clean house,
 and we wish for a tidy room,

Mother Earth prefers a wholesome place,
so all creatures can fully bloom.

Though conservation seems
a challenge,
it is not
beyond our reach.

"It's easy if we work together —
at home, around town, at the beach!"

Enjoy Earth's wonders every day.
Her beauty will spark a smile.

Plant a seed or tree.
Love your planet.
A lifelong project,
and so worthwhile.

A Dozen Things a Child Can Do For Earth

Save trees by saving paper.
Don't waste paper towels, napkins,
tissues or toilet paper.

Go for an "Eco" walk, picking up debris
along the way. You enjoy nature while
nature enjoys you!

When grandparents ask,
"What would you like for your birthday?",
impress them by asking for a tree!
Plant it somewhere special. The tree will clean the air,
and you will treasure it much longer than any toy.

Close doors and windows
when using heat or air conditioning.
It takes energy
to keep temperatures regulated.

Save water by taking shorter
showers and turning off
the water while
brushing your teeth.

Recycle beverage containers at sporting
events. Most likely, you will
get people thinking green and recycling
more themselves.

In the refrigerator and freezer,
find what you need,
and shut the door promptly.

TOWN OF
AURORA
RECYCLES

Limit time on electronics:
TV, computer and video games.
Lift your spirits by playing
outside instead.

See if your school recycles paper.
If not, inquire about starting a green club.

Turn off the lights when
you leave a room.

"Plant it for the planet."
Plant something every season with your
family. It's fun to plant a pumpkin seed in
the spring and harvest in the fall.

Live life according to the **3 Rs:**
Reduce (consumption)
Reuse (fix/repair items)
Recycle (waste, donate usable goods)

For more ideas visit:
www.onechildoneplanet.com